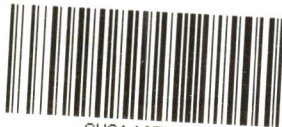

The Mystery Parcel

written by
Eric Charles

illustrations by
Shelagh McGee

GRAFTON BOOKS

A Division of the Collins Publishing Group

LONDON GLASGOW
TORONTO SYDNEY AUCKLAND

Grafton Books
A Division of the Collins Publishing Group
8 Grafton Street, London W1X 3LA

Published by Grafton Books 1986

© 1986 Brown Wells and Jacobs Limited. London

British Library Cataloguing in Publication Data

Charles, Eric
    The general store: the mystery parcel.—
    (The Village; 4)
    I. Title   II. Series
    823'.914[J]   PZ7
    ISBN 0-246-13070-9

It was the week before the village fête that Mr. Perkins, who ran the General Stores, found a mysterious parcel hidden away at the back of his shop. He took it down from the shelf and blew the dust from it. It had been there a long time and looked very old.

3

Mr. Perkins showed it to his wife.
"It's addressed to my grandfather when he ran the shop," he said.

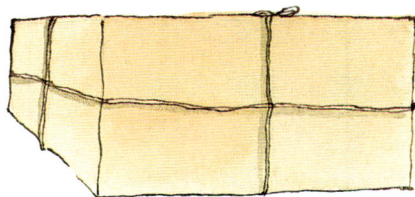

Mrs. Perkins shook the parcel. "I wonder what's inside it," she said. "It's a mystery," said Mr. Perkins. Then he had an idea. "If we don't open it, we could raffle it at the village fête as a mystery parcel."

"We could even ask people to try to guess what's inside it," said his wife.

Mr. Perkins put the unopened parcel in
the window of the shop with a notice
saying:

WIN THIS
MYSTERY
PARCEL
AT THE VILLAGE
FÊTE – Buy your
raffle tickets here

A. Perkins Esq.,
General Stores,
The Village.

The brown paper parcel with the old-
fashioned postage stamps caused a
lot of excitement in the village. People
came to stare at it in the General

Store's window, trying to guess what
was inside it. So many people came
into the shop to buy raffle tickets that
the old brass bell above the door broke
and Mr. Perkins had to fit an electric
buzzer instead.

When George Meadowcroft, the local
window-cleaner, came in to buy a raffle
ticket, he didn't like the sound of the

new buzzer.

"I prefer the sound of the old brass bell," he told Mr. Perkins. "You'll have to get yourself another one."

☆ ☆ ☆
MYSTERY
PARCEL
DRAW
WILL BE MADE
AT
4 O'CLOCK

On the day of the fête, Mr. Perkins set up his stall under the large elm tree. Mrs. Perkins decorated it with coloured ribbons, crêpe paper and spotted balloons. She put the mystery parcel in the middle of the stall above a notice which read, 'MYSTERY PARCEL DRAW WILL BE MADE AT 4 O'CLOCK'.

Then she went with Mr. Perkins for a walk round the fête.

Mr. Hudd, the baker, had made a wonderful display of fancy cakes and people were queuing up to buy them.

Mr. Spiggins,
the garage man,
was also having a
great success with his
tyre-hopping game.

13

At Farmer Wheatley's stall, his son Roggy had a giant marrow and people had to guess its weight. His friend Hannah wrote down their guesses on a sheet of paper.

Roggy banged a drum. "Roll up—roll up!" he shouted. "Guess the weight of the giant marrow!"

14

It was a fine day for a village fête
and everyone was enjoying themselves.

At four o'clock a large crowd gathered
around Mr. Perkins' stall, bursting with
curiosity to know what was inside the
mystery parcel.

Mr. Perkins put all the raffle tickets into a bucket and asked Holly Soames, the vicar's young daughter, to draw one out. She closed her eyes, put her hand in the bucket and drew out the winning ticket. Mr. Perkins looked at the number on the ticket and then announced "Number twenty-seven".

"ME!" shouted George Meadowcroft from the back of the crowd. "I've won the mystery parcel!"

Everybody cheered him.

16

Curious to know what was inside
the parcel, people crowded around
George as he slowly opened it.

When the last wrapping had been
carefully removed, he opened the box.

Inside was an old-fashioned brass
shop bell.

"Well, I'm blowed!"
exclaimed Mr. Perkins.
"All those years ago
my grandfather must
have ordered that bell
in case the one over the
door ever got broken."

"And it did," said George. He handed
Mr. Perkins the bell and said, "There you
are, Perky, put that above your shop
door. I can't stand the noise of that
electric buzzer thing."

 ZZZZZZZZZ!

"Well done, George," said the vicar. "It will be nice to hear the sound of a real shop bell again."

Then he turned and spoke to the
people gathered around.
 "Thank you, everybody, for making the
fête such a huge success. All the money
collected today will go towards the
cottage hospital fund." Everybody clapped.

21

"And who knows," continued the vicar, "maybe next year, Mr. Perkins will have another look at the back of his shop and find another mystery parcel to raffle!"

Get your own Village
Poster. Collect the
series and create
your own village!
See over for details.

To obtain your Village Poster please complete the details below then carefully cut this page along the dotted line.

Name _____

Address _____

_____

_____ Age _____

Send with a cheque or postal order (not cash) for £2.00, which includes post and packing, made out to —
Grafton Books Limited.

Marketing Department
Grafton Books
8 Grafton Street London W1X 3LA
Allow 28 days for delivery